Windfall

Windfall

Greg McLaren

PUNCHER & WATTMANN

First published in 2018
Published by Puncher and Wattmann
PO Box 279
Waratah NSW 2298

http://www.puncherandwattmann.com
puncherandwattmann@bigpond.com

ISBN   9781925780130

A catalogue record for this book is available from the National Library of Australia

Cover design by Miranda Douglas

Printed by Lightning Source International

This project has been assisted by the Australian Government through the Australia Council, its arts funding and advisory body.

Australian Government

Australia | Council
for the Arts

Contents

Windfall

Cockle Creek

From the Provinces

Windfall

Rainfall

after John Burnside

for Niobe Syme and Bonny Cassidy

The night breeze snores in the trees
and etches the sky with frogmouths.
Unlit cars fuss past the breathing window,
and drop down the valley road —

they cast streaked points of light
across jags of movement — bats, insects,
owls — and lend motion to letter-boxes,
fence-posts, ghost gums.

Light, persistent rain stills the bush
and its pale and sleepless ghosts
of trappers, trapped quolls, failed prospectors:
they unstitch what you know, but faintly.

Robert Adamson in *The Valley of Gwangi*

There are terrible reptiles we never quite catch
with our puny lassoes
we leave camp in the morning disguised as animals –
Eohippus, the dawn horse, or the bird-mimic, *Ornithomimus*

I never really believed it when I first laid eyes
on Gwangi, the living Allosaurus, trolling around the valley
It reminded me of my cousin skinny-dipping
in the river and eating raw fish

Eventually our horses will run away
and we'll be cactus, standing around like living fossils
on TV
while my Aunty Beryl watches

We are surrounded by "poems"
that seem to be making fun of us

Windfall

after Caroline Caddy

1.

It begins somewhere else,
       the drought that floats
              down the blue length

of seasons.
These roads are empty,
       they harvest silence
              from stretched and fenced-in crops

between breath from inland
       and the coast, far-off
              and flashing like a storm.

Beside the deserted cottage –
       is it? –
              the watertank's ribs

build barred shade across water's safe house.
       The country here's its own almanac,
              illustrated, legible, plain,

pages always flipped halfway to something –
       not reward, or demand;
              fitful, itself, nothing else.

2.

Drought is here from inland,
          erasing its own marks.
Is it autumn? winter?

Roads harvest distance —
          what might be crops
breathe the soil's dark water.

The iron roof —
          pages of a calendar,
or flapping like a beggar's frock.

3.

Rainbow lorikeets from below —
                    bright, upturned chevrons.

Winter is a dying,
          warmth dripping from your bones
                    in the stiff sunshine.

You drive hours, then,
          to pass by your old house
where the dog was,
          decades behind, and died.

This is the sweetest birth,
          with you, this new thing.

We slide so near the past
                    soft and ancient now,
through red shift, blue shift: never still.

They could almost belong

After Sarah Holland-Batt

She's gone now, the little green Mirage hissing out
into the night as I keep turning over the riff
to *Final Twist*, falling into the buzzing ring of chords.
My fingers are callused; there's weed across from the neighbours;
some bickering down the stairwell; the fluoro overhead's
winking into a migraine – the aura around everything
that comes; the flat's light's muddy, a cheap Rembrandt print.
Fruit bats are in at the landlord's mandarins. Nothing
appears or vanishes, not really, not here in Bellbird.

At Seven Mile Beach

After Chase Twichell

Last xmas lunch the talk round the barbie
the three men had commandeered, working close
in the heat, but pointedly not touching,

was conspiratorial. Literally. You
don't want or need me to join the dots.

I offered drinks and talked a sec, offhand,
about the long weather. Chortles and guffaws,
stiff fuck mes in shaking undertones.
                                        So.
Can you imagine, then, the abandoned piles
of longnecks, some of them shattered,

the vines, the long stretch of morning glory, twining
up and over the bbq, the outdoor setting, the wisteria's bones
tendrilled across the deck? The pool, kidney-shaped, drained

or evaporated, veined with splits and filling with plant litter, silt of air,
animal corpses.
                At Seven Mile Beach, the wind's up.
Our daughter's out along the stinging strand,

collecting shells in her red castle bucket, one
of each type she can find – sea- and sand-worn,
smoothed-over
                as a neat bed, say, in a hospice.

The animals – scallops, pipis, oysters, the hermit
crabs,

where are they? Where did they go?
But the wind – the wind driving the little grits of sand

south in a fine low mist a thermal then catches
and lifts, blends with salt spray, as the crescent
scoops around a mile on or more, rising in a broad haze

but the wavelets on the surface, tiny patterned dunes,
move but don't seem to shift – and here

the slow enormous sea too slides itself in,
pushing its jagged pane in, unfurling,

perpendicular to the wind,
the sand's sharp and brilliant array.

There, there's a rip, just there,
see it, sweetie?, that still-seeming,
flattened water.

            Looks safe,
but I'd rather risk a whirlpool.

A scatter offshore of dark rocks,
seal-coloured and dashing under the white –
the land's old bones left after

the long round green hills've ground to thin sand,
crab-burrowed then, barnacled.

When we leave, when we're gone, what
will we be taking with us? What'll we leave?

The sun's fat orange blaze cramps in behind
Berry Mountain, the air around the streets
have been rich with wood smoke
these last days of autumn.

What else?
Gone means all of us, doesn't' it, gone
like a child smashed to the road;
or ripped out by the hard sheeting water and fish-eaten; or

burnt but first gagged and choked in that
damp pressing heat caught in the locked
back room we thought was safe.
                          Flashing in the speeding light
angled off cars, fixed to a huge swamp mahogany

with helices of tape – floral memorials
to the dead from prangs on local roads, and just
around the long and shaded corner

is Harley Hill, the bush cemetery there,
its paths in heavy shade but mown
and chopped through scrub by council:

here's little Pearl Amelia Boorman,
aged two, died February 1910.

That's an end, sure, but not the end.

These crabs in their grass-topped dunes
flit, as clouds, into burrows,
eclipse themselves with dark sand

shaded by late-on-the-scene she oaks.
Here's a plastic bottle, half-submerged;

translucent microbeads rolling with the breeze
in the sand, so like it, indistinguishable; a cough mixture bottle,
label half-faded; an interstate number plate

rusts in the carpark's shade,
where feral chooks rough up
the leaf litter.
           When I'm

eclipsed, elapsed, by this cancer, or by
whatever, when we're all done in and done for,
these slight shells, their animals:

won't they still pivot into the earth
at the hover of gulls, the grey
rattle of herons diversifying,

and taking on new tastes, chasing
the crabs down their broad sandy whirlpools?

Suppose something, sooner or
later, will do that.

The wind. It's insistent.

At night, driving

After Derek Mahon

I bolt through in the night-wet Falcon
past the graveyards at Sandgate, street-
& traffic-lights buzzing away at the thin
soft rain lacquering the mangroves,
the windows and rooves alongside,
and past, then, the silent steelworks
shaken by geology, shares, demography,
resentful of what was there and of
what's there now, the change-over of shifts
gone to dusty statuary, the civic palms
in the forecourt there shed fluoro shade
across bare cement creased with grassy rails.
That smell of burning fuel and of asphalt
in summer's early arvos has extinguished
itself, maybe. Too much arson around.
That city's gone. It did itself in
with blunt forgetting, tunnelled
under and gouged away.
                              When the sun
comes back, or the moon phases over,
waves offshore kiss and spray the outline
brilliantly, a patient weightless mist.
It'll only vanish and return, which is nothing.

Poems the size of Les Murray

1.
There's a woman in the Union Hotel front bar
drinking Reschs. On the jukebox,
Hank Williams – *There's a Tear in my Beer*.

2.
There's a bloke in Martin Place
drinking metho to wash away
the taste of the VB he'd started on.

3.
That mulleted kid in winklepickers
ordering Beam and coke
at Kurri Workers knows better.
It'll end in.

4.
There's a big man in the shade
of some Bulahdelah café
wheezing on his Samsung,
talking Sanskrit to his cows.

5.
Sum dude bawln martn pl
check it
#wont stop #stfu #fag

Sprung

After Gig Ryan

Downstairs, raised voices,
percussion on flesh.
The garden's currawongs wolf-whistle.

His glittering nose in the foyer
among the unswept and the cats' piss.
His other 's glazed quiet, her near air numb.

Light spirals in around off the street;
durry-strewn, the glassy shopfronts across.
First headlights splash them, and the last.

The glow from unspecied trees, collated in the bark,
slips. The wind through them sounds out
a verdict. The room was smaller than it'd seemed.

The Kurri Kurri Book of the Dead

after Charles Wright

for Mark Mahemoff

1.

Thursday night, mid-November,
shopping dockets replenish dead money.
Vertical blinds divide the near-full moon seen through a gauze

of darkened cirrus; a pair of koels past midnight, harrassed by mynahs.
Their trill spins, rolling into the night.
The kitchen tap washer is just about gone –

a water clock: finitude ticks
and anxiety spills out.

Sitting by Heathcote Creek, a little shaded,
casting my own shadow across it,
as the yellow-tailed black cockatoos cark and sigh,
all I think of is skin,
                    how it administers love.
This closed-in landscape
                         is a bulb's captured and half-
imagined flash, folded away, the wind leaking in.

How far and how easily I've drifted –
to look at your life
                    is like watching tv through frosted glass.
These are cells that exist to divide.
Is the moon waxing? Is it waning?
The night always stretches and drags impossibly.
                                        So what?

I've spent half the day on this flat rock above water
sketching the outlines of *Corymbia, Angophora* –
lost eucalypts, they trail the sun with their leaves.

Suppose the blue gums across Mt Sugarloaf between Kurri
and the lake
    are still there:

2.

Armistice Day afternoon, back in Kurri a day.
I stand at the rotunda's memorial, my uncle George's voice
in my head, soldierly, as I try to still
      my family's forgetting.

Light adheres – to the asphalt new-laid
on potholes down Hopetoun Street,
      to the white duco on that LC Torana,
to the stubbie perched on the bin,
to the leaves of acacia, oleander, grevillea,
      fence-side rose shrubs, each
clipped with a portioned sun.
Trail bikes trap and amplify stirred-up bees in scrub
past the sub-station, where ozone-sweet air hangs,
then drifts in a mood.
     December and January's high slang of bushfire smoke?
Six weeks off, a calendar page that flaps in a hot wind,
      impatient almanac
of green shoots from black ashed surfaces of the hushed bush,
its birds poured out, an empty jar.
     Lewisham,
      I mutter,
fucken Lewisham, where night homes in now.
It's not home: home is where dread sat,

where pale tea clatters, crumbs random on the pale tablecloth
that fills with mauve light from the west —

                                 Canterbury, Cessnock, wherever.

On the way in the bus driver pulled over, marking the silence,
but confused the old and dateless loves.

3.
Is the moon waxing or waning?
Writing The Kurri Kurri Book of the Dead again

                                     as I near a

birthday —
the moon's an ulcer,

                      its light a bright sepsis.
It glows in the drunk scrawl on the back steps

                            of a snail after rain.
From this angle, the mucus is pure silver,
the steps have been there forever.

                      *

Parto was cracking on about bourbon, bikers
and Vikings. He was fucked-up

                      on something or other,
out front of his tattoo joint. I didn't have a clue.
All I knew is the moon does something,

                      even as
it dulls the stars out and blanks the dark. His face erased
with a pipe bomb. What he did wrong, he'll never set right,
even if he'd wanted to —

the dry northerly scours this away, weak and relentless,
into the silence past Mt Tumblebee, the wind's through the gums,

a sudden ocean tide that drops, exhales, drops,
strange even now.

                    Was anything ever clear. South of here,
two hundred yards beneath Richmond Main, the abandoned mines —
all that deep coal submerged, a faint splashing,

                                    you suppose, unheard.

4.

Slurping VBs at the Chelly, Wednesday afternoon.
The low sun mellows the pub's red bricks

                           plastered with 50s
tiled league cameos — Newtown, North Sydney, Balmain.
We all went down to Montreux

                    on the Lake Geneva shoreline —

tinny from the jukebox, a tributary of treble and gank.
You walk over, between the laminex tables, slip in a coin, and we leave.

I don't know they'll love Joni Mitchell.

The Chelmsford's scrubbed from the rearview,
Roy Orbison's on in your green Lancer —

                        you're singing along,
I'm not — *Running Scared*, and then
Paul Kelly (*he who is nothing*

                  will suddenly come into view).
Their bodies sing, *every muscle aching*, of bodies
beneath theirs, or distant past time.

                      My hands never knew
what to do when you were dancing.

Look — the late sun on the paperbarks,

                    the blackbutts and the blue gums.

You ask about the chitter dump we've just passed – those rank coal tailings,
offcuts and discards, half a mile behind the house on Cessnock Road,
and I tell you about summer days
on the front verandah watching the wooden coal carts
piled with sunny black,

                             returning late and empty from the harbour,
a forgetting circle,

                 below the night's blunt outline over Neath hill.

5.

Wiping my fingers, greasy after lunch, on my jeans
and a Sudanese boy, maybe ten,

                      clangs a rhythm
with a stick on the slippery-dip behind Kurri baths.
Filaments from paperbark blossoms, a light spray

                            across the seat and bench,
tagged *earn.one*, over and over with a slim white posca on green.
The wind runs semi-tones, begins a scale in the casuarinas.

This, then, is spring,

                this one's headed full-pelt now for summer –
I should be indoors, I should be kinder to myself
but vacancy, loathing, the life I left behind here,

                       they clack over and reset.
The car's just over there.
I could go.

                    *

Carol the librarian lets me into local history,
but I've got no questions.

                  This lightness, no-one
knowing you're here – you don't know why, but you think

of a bee over a front yard dotted with clover.
The pages mumble with dates and names that mean something to the dead.

Kurri skims across the library's window –

you step out and cross the road
to the takeaway. Scallops and chips, with vinegar. A coke.
Civic Park, downwind of the rotunda, its hymn

of war dead,
durries and coal dust –
there, two kids, half-arsed emos,

his arm half up her shirt,
her hair blue, exactly the sky's colour. The wind moves like a hand.

6.
Haven't you finished with the place yet?

Full moon, a week shy
of December, and no-one's arms to lean into.
There's a cloudbank – silvery cumulus – probably just west of Cessnock.
Walking past the school's early lights,

a boy's rilling through scales,
then houses of once-pastel fibro, corrugated tin.

A mower.

A phone rings and a voice comes on through the fly-wire.
Past the shops, a squat woman with a plastic bread tray.
Down laneways, the flush of toilets and showers

burble
and rush through the town
toward the sewage works in the bush between Northcote Street and Alcan.
Windows flicker with televised colour, and shake. Nobody's in them.

*

I overhear footy talk in the cake shop
but don't know the names —

         twenty years spent in Sydney.
They're in third spot on the table, behind Maitland and Lakes.

Shit.
The snort of liniment and vinegar at the graveyard's kiosk —
the right words tear out the years: you haven't left yet.

On looking into Pam Brown's *Selected*

It's a Lewisham mid-afternoon,
clear-skied mid-winter. In the park,
reading poetry and a British non-
photographer's history
of American photography.
There are children
running noisily between the trees,
bored with the see-saw,
the roundabout, the sandpit.
Page nineteen of Pam's *Selected Poems 1971-
1982* is − wow − a palimpsest!
At the start of the poem,
she quotes Ginsberg, and,
pencilled-in below, is − *poet*.
They have circled Pam's *benzedrine / tequila*,
and scrawled beneath, also circled, *drug*
and *alcohol*. The children's father
is naming the eucalypts to his wife,
and she calls to the kids: *Jaiden! Brianna!*
Back to the table! Their shadows lengthen.
CASSADY IS DEAD,
Pam declaims, and our reader,
the book's first owner,
has inscribed: *Pop star (cult heroes − drugs, etc)*.

Late, romantic

after Rainer Maria Rilke

There's a myth riding on this,
visible as her body below you,
it glows, damp, full of breathing.
Your eyes are everywhere, your voice low

and you well with blood, love, quickness.
Nothing distracts you; nothing to
distract you. You're hip-on-thigh,
in the dark summered bedroom,

hard as, your face a translucent thing.
Somehow it kisses or licks a shoulder
that gleams, a flood of animal bone

beneath borderless skin
coming apart. You know, blindly,
there's nothing left to change.

Table

after Rosemary Dobson

On the picnic table, merlot and,
with a bright condensation ring, Coopers green —
and wind over and through our poems,
whispering them into the angophora.

Melaleuca pollen dusts the crossword
half-done, printed on felled forest
near Canberra, tiered, arrayed,
almost a landscape.

A few pages escape. They rise
and litter the harbour cove
below, transforming the ink
into another darkened fluid.

Childhood trauma

after John Tranter

1.

They burn the radio, they listen to the blue.
The okapi farmers whisper
at their meetings, and skirt the gardens.
Their articles revel in a cultural effect.
A multiple connection is enough,

I suppose; it's a way to influence cool.
They want ordination in that religion
practiced by Bolivians. If they
retreat too soon from danger, they'll be
unable to explain magic. And any

attraction is important: it's a kind of high.
Smooth groups of comrades criticise
their elders' speech, so full of *faux pas* –
superiority provokes confidence.

2.

The automobile industry makes sense
when you're smoking joints in the dunes.
Your decision to get breakfast at the café
overlooking the beach was a good one.

We're flanked by metallic heat and sound —
don't push it. You set yourself against
your family, it leaves you feeling light,
and elusive as fish. I'm against it,

but supportive. Cloud ships over, and then
rain stains the wall of the rock that we
descend into the lagoon-side quarry.

I meant to say what you needed to hear.
Everything usually goes unsaid.
I needed a family, but found none.

3.

The drunk swindler falls from the bus,
a happy impact. His briefcase of ethics
readings was featured in the newspaper —
his GP and lawyers weren't happy.

But isn't the conscious desire to change stupid?
Assuming everything has purpose, as if
expecting a film to improve with viewing?
How soon the city turns into a national economy.

That's how it worked in the book, with its
estimations that flit from topic to topic, isn't it?
Or is it still stupid, though you love its capacity

for morality, while that pissant turd, affecting
honour, looking down your top as the bus
pulls up, becomes painfully enamored of you?

4.

We laugh at ourselves with some difficulty,
but it's not impossible to create a system
to analyse our later moods. The photograph
we stuck to the fridge was removed

by the visiting International Socialist.
Time's incisions cut across your deepest thoughts,
and inevitably a complex answer builds up
from our conditioned methodology.

We hold and burn next year's calendar,
the chemicals warp from the photos
and the lost dates appear again, valuable,

capacious. Love is nothing but today. This
pursuit of loss chews at my paragraphs.
Through the fast later years, we know we'll know less.

5.

The woman falls in love's slow reduction.
Except for the window, all is movement
through winter's fog. It grows dark,
so they donate a baptismal.

Compressed time is a sad mother
who calls in at your mental home.
*Mate, these women just pounded around
the power station in the downwards dark;*

*and have you seen the girls who preen themselves
nervously in the heat? We'll have 'em squealing.*
The bandits fall in with fanatics, but they

want only to pet the animals suffering
in the Caribbean dirt. Rain is soft,
it inclines tenderly – your harem of weather stops.

6.

Does being the subject
of innumerable paintings
mean the child is weighted
down by arts administrators?

You need to make a call.
The train moves the boy
shifting his entire sky,
which is only history.

A soldier intones the wind
as he takes another train
to deplorable borders,
to reveal what it is to punish —

the lesion revives, and the boy hides
in the completed painting of the sky.

7.

The edge of the afternoon returns
to itself. Winter disfigures the ground
with its fallen matter, the strange
tired flippancy of corruption.

It is worn-out before it started,
but presses further, an introspective child.
The radio blurts vague, waffled policy,
reserved for people satisfied

in the sick and blackened cities,
as, at last, they turn over the rocks
beached along the shore. There's.
a feeling of increase in the stations,

ascending then gone. He thinks:
when he swims, he's really there.

8.

They are courageous, even if it is induced.
Your fellow passengers climb down
the scales of water as you work through
from childhood to deviation.

That old requirement goes too far.
If you deploy the whole of memory,
you might sleep, though it's the source of un-
restricted pain. However you press on,

death's inside that promise, too: the gauge
is overheated, we're too detached,
everything is a bad film where we worry

away our wealth on simplicity, where the light
gets stranger, somebody writes, lights up,
and our time with the bottle turns so wrong.

Kurri 1977

after J.S. Harry

it's thirty seven
years ago

abandoned coal seams still snake far below
the concrete and couchgrass

silence glistens
in the schoolyard chatter

        someone
isn't at school today

that's two
        someone else
        knows something

he dresses
for the dole office

behind the clothing factory
in that long grass

is Darren Fisher
patient as sunlight

he breathes ants

The Wheelbarrow variations

after William Carlos Williams and A. R. Ammons

> high-falutin
> language does not
> rest on the
> cold water
> all night
> by
> the luminous
> birches

A. R. Ammons, *Tape for the Turn of the Year.*

1.

the morse-code
of magpies

does everything
to keep

winter's sunless
mood disorder

at bay   their white
on black

2.

so   the deep-end
of this

river pool
's narrow

we lazed away
        our daughter

beside the white
ghost gums

3.

not a thing
language does
is at rest
like still water
on an upturned
steel bucket
with a gum leaf
in it

4.
so much light
falls upon

the red-green
lorikeets

glinting and still
above the white fiat

5.
What depends
on the red wattlebird

quaking the blossoms
of the grevillea

in the front yard
between the sleepers?

6.
So. What
the fuck

is the big deal
about

glazed rain
water

and a couple
of white boilers?

Hey, Bill,

forgive me   for burning
the ice in the vial

I was fucked up   like a plum
and it looked so   umm   icy

Have ya got a dollar fr a pack
a smokes?

                         I'll cut ya.

Edge

after Bruce Beaver

The galahs have got it sussed —
summer's light, and light on, its grey-pink plenty
down to its last, and they go,
as the gulls' immaculate taste
snaps at air, and chips, as their
rank call praises all scraps
snatched from beneath figs, palms, shadecloth.
Galah feathers are windfall leaves,
mite-flavoured and air-light fruit —
the sky lifts, swallows and disgorges
the plumage like pips.
They gather on the grass and harvest laughter.
The sky is a thick threat of clouds
that shunt the sky from their darkening channels:
the hard compressed air fluffs wings
as it buffets, cools and argues with the warm.
The galahs notice — they're hard-wired and bird-wise —
and start to move on, with their yellow combed relations.
Over the golf course and beach parks and carparks,
autumn drifts in on its replenishing gulls.

Into evening

After Simon West

The wind-blunted laurels and gums.
Rain buffs the orange tree leaves
in our bedroom window in silver-lead light,
impossible to know what time.

Smell of coast. In another room, The Saints,
Brisbane (Security city), *Prehistoric Sounds*, not
dulled by walls and closed doors.
The rain's electrical, the sky feels close

as if hail is imminent. The tree looks somehow
Chinese-y against the cream-coloured bricks
next door, all rivers and mountains, falling into
all the space there is, forever, or my idea of Du Fu's or

Wang Wei's idea of it. Leaves, tremulous
as D.T. hands. The clouds probably build and pile,
build and pile in the dark, where I know the trapdoor's
smooth burrow glistens. Her forelegs barely tap

at the couchgrass, feeling at the earth there, crouched
maybe patiently; certain something will carry her way
in the thickening air. Lighting, illuminated alfoil.
It's silent a long time.

White-faced heron

After Judith Beveridge

Crooked River's tidal this close
to the sharp wind's Pacific. Stone-
still, among cragged oysters, dipping,
stalking pale shadow, lost as you

look away, found squinting again,
neck waving the way bobbed wind makes
the reeds move in these small cool gullies
of rush, spattering the river's

silvery twist of neck, scalloping
bright thousands of shells, just as the coast
road tears through the flat few *k*s of dark
arched blackbutt, of sand-sound bangalay,

the shining black curves, they fatten
and taper, curl away into
the late sun's needling light, the fade
overhead now loose grades of sky, of cloud.

Utterance

after Tracy Ryan

for Frankie

The day you were born,
your great-uncle George,
ten years dead, cheerful,
round-faced, sallow,

slid behind your face
as you began to fill it –
his a short phrase
your pursed uneven mouth

couldn't utter long.
                              Birth,
always a slow marriage
to someone's death.

The time your mother
took to shower clean
that first clear morning
pressed and spread a vast

now that continues.
Your fast slowing heart
is retrieved from the worst
of terrors, and held against mine,

your dark eyes aimless at first
and full of search.
We try to look at each other
and our gaze doesn't fail.

Cockle Creek

The Du Fu variations

On the *Narrabeen*, thinking of AusLit

The wind lifts, it's cold, and you wonder
if or where the sky ends.

Koels from the far north flood your sleep
as inland rivers spill over, for once: early spring.

Your great poems sink, not sing, and
the harbour's sharks dine on their drowners:

our nation scribbles lines to dead swagmen
and drunks. Are we a bit twitchy? Why would that be?

Spring scene

The government's fallen, the mountains and hinterland
burn. Rivers silt. Grass is thick in the old

cities' streets. Pollen falls and catches
on the breeze. Here and there birds

startle and cry. Fires are flares at night
all spring. I could write ten thousand

letters home, or postcards. My worried hair
so thin – where in fuck's that hat?

Dreaming of Li Po

i.m. Noel Rowe

I choke on grief,
though it belongs to you.
There's nothing else.
Where you are, I can't know.

I snag glimpses of you
down King Street, in Norton
Plaza, but no longer
in dreams. You're not here —

so far from the Nambucca River
shore, its mangroves. It's night
that closes around the fence-lines,
shrouding your return, or anyone's.

It's splashed on the tin roof,
the moon is, and I nearly see you.
In the dark, the water is shockingly
deep. Please, be safe.

The New Christs and Du Fu at world's end

The nation's in hell, but there are still mountains,
and the rivers make their run to the sea
past the dogs and the flies. I swear birds gargle
and talk through the light-bleached wattle

off Wardell Road. Someone famous died —
it's trending. A whole year of them.
We need money to feed the kid: what to wear
to the interview? Suit with a tie, without the tie?

Six variations

1.

The sun boils from the sea and rises,
on the heat, behind a draught of clouds. Below,
a sacred kingfisher, opal-still, its shadow
branch-snagged above Cowan Creek.

2.

Pollen, gum blossoms, tonal thrum of bees —
they weave and spread across spring's first weeks.
Sitting cross-legged, waiting for the bus,
reading Tony Harrison, wanting only quiet.

3.

Braided rain tumbles through the rust-busted
gutter – no budget for repairs.
Stuck leaves spit out and spill – old boats
run aground, they fade to a rumour of stains.

4.

Late afternoon electrical storm spent now, cracked
wide with low sun – see the paperbarks hum
with light, with currawongs. They obsess over song,
a brief psalm. Corellas flash by, busted-open white.

5.

Paspalum spills under the fence, a banana tree
next to the driveway. The grassy footpath
sodden, we walk greyhounds on the shining road,
their nails knitting the dusk as it hovers a while.

6.

Full moon on the wet shed roof.
The old creek is a concreted ditch.
Dad – *There's an owl.* A frogmouth.
The smell of rain. Will we ever be home?

The moon above my brother

Convoys out from Singleton barracks – we pull over
in the country grass. Shushing the silence, a string of plovers

pulled tight as wire that sings. They reflect in headlit dew –
small thin crescents, bobbing: the autumn moon above our old
        house.

My brother – where is he? Email abbreviates the letters
we've no time to write to short epistles about his niece.

He posts photos of Brunswick Heads on Facebook. I've
never been there. North Korea mutters something about war.

What got seen

Frost in the gardens of Abermain, Weston, Neath.
Under the bridge, tracks have dulled – the coal fifty years
gone, grunted out from under the dark, pouring with dust
that settled on sheets and windows miles off.

The railway pubs are still left – they wait on bankrupting
        reno quotes
or foreclosure. History's a drive-past and a smudged
photostat map. I rode out to the horizon, past Sawyers,
even, every day, looking out toward the edge of the world.

Thinking of my son

1.

Never met, did we? Magpies
curl sound around spring – spring
which is always a green suddenness,
or seems it. You wouldn't know – how

could you, little blind stub. Rivers and mountains
forever. Trees accumulate rings.
It's cold, tonight. I'd forgotten you.
I'm up late,
                listening to my daughter sleep.

2.

It's spring, now, little bear.
We've been apart
                so long.
Do you hear lorikeets,
as they strip the light, where you are?

I weary – the seasons and years
don't slow down.
                To not see
your tall shadow against a doorframe, to not
watch you stomp and slip across shaded
creeks.
                In the sun filled with traffic and birds,
and about to doze into the redbrick wall,
your mother nowhere I know,
                    something
shifts in the magnolia.
                I almost see you.

Mines

Something pale and blunt is in the dying jacaranda.
Mice, or worse, from the long grass next door.
Long before Rothbury, people died here by the hundred.
A dim light down the road – telegraph poles are dark, erect bones.

Drinking

Didn't John Forbes sell lotto?
Who nearly jumped from Varuna?

You're better off dying, or retiring young –
even to Dapto or Leichhardt. Maybe.

Anyway. What good's writing poetry,
if Bill Williams and Jann Harry are dead?

Get less morbid – if we still can draw breath,
let's crack out the Codral and Jameson's.

Spring

The country we thought we knew
is gone. But its harbour-mouthed rivers
still drain from the steady low mountains.

Exclusion zones and quarantined towns
are busy with grass, spread thin and wide
as cattle ribs that whole long drought. Tall lights

scan perimeters − wind-blown blossoms, spot fires −
and sirens spin through the night like alarmed
plovers, disoriented junkies, horny koels.

It's hard, still, to get through to people.

Eucalypts along the Cooks River

1.
Earlwood's blossoming melaleucas
are maddening − I can't explain

how much I love their scent,
their texture.

I crank up the PC
to check whatpaperbarkami.com.au

I tried the url three or four times
and got only 404: page not found.

2.

These tendrils burst – supernovas –
and spill into the river, the mangroves.

I need to sit down –
this spring staggers me.

There's only poems left, and walking,
to do. Don't

pity me –
look up: the ironbarks' rusting bloom.

3.

Houses backed onto the Cooks
breathe in the mangroves and she-oaks –

further along, toward Tempe,
the butter-smell of paperbarks in flower,

charms me back into, I don't know. What?
What do I do? What can I do.

Hey, summer –
I spilled my Hollandia on your grass!

4.

In the mountains
Winmalee's gums are ash.

and they fall on Marrickville
leaf by leaf.

Who could afford
to rebuild — the premiums

through the roof, if the roof's
still standing, that is.

5.

Across the Cooks — the Earlwood mangroves.
Silt's a living grave

the low afternoon light flops across.
Breeze flaps the sunlight there,

native bees sup at splayed gum nuts,
the spilt pollen's wind drops.

Bits of flowers float in Steel Park's water play
where toddlers pick at them.

6.

The council's let the gums
go — shed branches and bark

everywhere, bleeding flowers
and that salt smell. There are no

Christmas beetles stuttering between
these trees, though pied currawongs

and magpies trade riffs
through the fading light. That's something.

7.

They'll blossom again
along the river's slow artery

filling it with soft colour
and light – fluid

through a canula
seen in late afternoon sun.

They'll press themselves open,
honey and dust spilling over,

Insurgents

Bridges

Dirty Toyota utes hack and wheeze
with murderers riding shotgun

away from the drone-buzzed camp,
ploughing dust and wind and sand

across the paths and bridges
their non-religionists met them on

weeks ago, pulling at their coats,
pushing the warm barrels aside,

the panic emptying to the wide
white sky closing in.

The front

We bury the IEDs, reach
for the nearest AK and wait

to take out the lead truck's tyres
first, and watch for the pop of mines

as the pricks get out.
Leave the longest beard for last.

North

1.

I pick across
the still and windy suburbs

The smell of wet ash —
no smoke now   no fire.

People are deformed,
or tattooed with blood

Ignore street-signs
keep an eye on high ground

avoid company
stay out of the open

leave it behind —
use the slow and brown river

thought it slaps and pisses
in the cliff-shade

The city's last jacarandas bloom early —
you could slip on the mauve sludge

This is an old road
its shoulder falls

into the hills   In their tight mist
panic's everything

but there's nothing
to be done with it

These berries — what
are they?   red

and black, darkened green,
soaked with thick light

and the dusty rain we get
not to be trusted

In that dream   I'm always
here   never moving on

What've I ever done
that wasn't a mistake?

2.

From here   the next range across
lumped with hills

and valleys   rough scars
time and water have jagged through

In bare light   the river
drips below   the worst of it behind

Frogmouths go quiet
in their waterlogged melaleuca

the long grass and reeds
drizzle with movement

Half-dark   this open forest
alongside the fenced-in water

the moon rises fat   swollen through trees
every surface is polished bone

There was a settlement here   once —
fire   flood   money   virus

distant bombs   emptied the district
built the silence   the forgetting

Uprising

after Wang Wei

1.

A thousand suburbs burning — who
would ever vote Liberal again.
Parliament's flagpoles — bare as forests.
Past Greenacre, is that gunfire, still? Queen's Birthday?

2.

I stayed offline til the election was way due
after Parliament was suspended.
It's not smart to see anyone, only
the moon, only Du Fu. This bloodwood.

3.

The people living here now — who are they?
Only the Cooks, draining past Tempe.
What's left to ask anyone as the rivers,
mountains, the bush and cities still empty out?

4.

Fuck, I hate these new sirens.
Someone's done for every time.
Kids, war-weary, play AFP.

All these suburbs — "South-West Sydney".
I feel my ulcer tighten, and think
at what travels down the rivers.

5.
Every day I'm not arrested or dead,
I rejoice that spring will recoil.
The abandoned pharmacy's a blessing –
why sorrow as they round up the Cabinet.

6.
Punchbowl's quiet as, block
after block browned-out and still.

Yesterday, sun on the clouds' pedestal –
a gagged body's pushed from a van.

In shop windows, only
the street's unpeopled other side.

Johnny Cash in my head
singing *Rambling Man, Solitary Man.*

An armoured freight train
passes, dull with camo and grease.

7.
He changes the government every second election
and every fortnight surveys the nation.
His editor-in-chief arrives, again,
but unionists surround the Parliament.
Some snow melt downhill from the foxholes –
the only smoke's from burning *Australian*s.

Cockle Creek

for my family

Off you go, then

It begins as a spring, or a leak from rocks
when rain spatters a crease raised in the shade

of the Sugarloaf Range past Killingworth. Whipbirds
in there drip uneven intervals among the blue gum.

after Wang Wei

1.
Ungala Road

That scratch-built squat Poppy built between
wars on reclaimed land behind the dunes is carpark
now, where kids in togs scoff at their parents —
keeping an eye on the talent, the time and the sunscreen.

2.
Rhondda hills

Wrens and, I suppose, finches, weave
this wide hillside scrub autumn — for millennia.
I've been over these ridges and tracks all
my life, walking this dark, breathing out griefs.

3.

These slim, slight gums shade the grey soil
but there's no shelter, and, ripe with pollen and spores,
rain plops and skitters through. They need this wet
on the divide's other side, not here.

4.
Lakeside

Tall wet eucalypts like bright poles step down
to their brittle reflection in the windscreen –
parked here near dusk just out of sight of the road,
not sure I've read my grandfather's map correctly.

5.
Billy Goat Hill and cemetery

No-one's here on this windless ridge
wedged above Booragul and Teralba.
It's late afternoon, and low light
pricks at the ti trees, the dusty melaleuca.

6.

Tile rooves and flame trees redden in this last
autumn light. One plover, and another, beyond the hill –
the sun glints on green. Wood-smoke
streaks and fades in the dark: then, only its smell.

7.

Red berries bleed from the green —
early spring again, the seasons a spinning blade.
Can walking across these hills
again be enough?

8.
Angophora

Above the shoreline, red-fleshed angophoras
drink the sun in; their moored shadows shift, so quiet,
across the dirt path the Council or Parks
keep in good nick in case of royalty or poets.

9.
Pulbah Island, 1972

The run-about's Evinrude outboard gags and purrs
fuel stink. We slip south halfway across the lake
to Pulbah Island — above the high tide mark, our picnic
amid ants, petrol, Paterson's Curse.

10.

Wangi jetty, Christmas, late afternoon. BBQ smell.
The lake's a crisp wide pane of frosted glass.
On the other shore, Swansea — boxed with houses, speckled
with caravans, cake shops, my grandparents' last home.

11.

i.m. Jody Thompson

Caravan park radio spits and lisps Slim Dusty into dusk.
The Thompsons, sun-drunk, hooroo back to Bellbird
as, if we'd turn from the lake to look, the Watagans behind
us unfurl clouds from inland like a beach-towel, or a shroud.

12.

A splash of willows beside Cockle Creek near
the junkyard and the turn-off to Teralba –
here's the row of sheds and streetlights
that funnels workers down hot asphalt to the Sulphide.

13.

King tide, June, rain all night, the Channel breakwater
under foam and splayed weed the length of Coon
Island. Wake from a returning trawler boils white.
The boat's port lights tremble, buoyant and green.

14.

Drink at the Great Northern? – shit,
no-one *respectable* ever did, she always said,
although that jade-tinted public bar stank of Ardath,
and overflowed with Resch's and KB.

15.

Past the Mine Rescue Station there, the slow-
moving creek gags on reeds and heavy metal effluent,
but when the Sulphide's stink's not up, come watch
the moon afloat with fish on the silver water.

16.

Here near the lake's northern wash into mangroves and wetland,
lights clang red at the crossing where trains clack south,
inland from green-caped bays and inlets studded with fences
and backyard boat ramps, where Dora Creek spills out foamy into
green.

17.
Valiant

for my grandparents

Sitting in the white Valiant's back seat that night,
country music on your radio, waking as trucks pass –
their lights splash and fill the car. In those hills again,
the moon covers me. I wish you were here to see.

18.
Wangi Wangi Caravan Park, 1971

Xanthorrhea and bottlebrush lift above scraps of understorey
burnt-though last summer, red on green on black, everywhere
around grey squat pillboxes, barred shut, never used, deep with leaf
litter, with twigs that crack underfoot like fire, or warfare.

19.
Frank

His parents' old green weatherboard house, at the end
of the street, in all-day hill-shade – forgotten by the State,
he never started school, or spoke. We saw him, once,
following sunlit drifts between the ridge-top gums.

20.
Davey Gunn

for my great grandmother

It must've been just after she'd died, their house, mapped-
out anew by visitors with plates and beer. A one-legged man
I stared at, and who soothed me, his breath all whisky
and stories I'd never remember, only their rhythm, a tone.

Coda

Past Edgeworth, the road in returns from forgotten dark.
No more hawkers or milkos selling from carts or out

the back of vans, pressing their work hard in against sunset
and dawn. All time between has been sleep-fuzz – but the house,

smaller now, with its red-tin roof. The wisteria's still there,
colouring the patio in, and the smell of burnt metal.

Smoke from the National Park bronzes the sun's small coin.
One last blurred look, and the warm gate sings shut behind.

After Wang Wei

1.

No-one to see, in these empty hills,
only far-off voices, or old echoes of voices.

Deep in the bush, sinking light
shines on the green tree-moss.

2.

Watching angophora blossoms fall
through dusk. This path — no-one on it
to alarm the understorey's lizards and birds.
Below here, a creek, or birds, chuckle.

3.

UTS — the poets reference
each other and exchange methodologies.
Far off Marrickville, staring into the distant
city, only a grey tower, wreathed with smoke.

Berry

Corellas scratch at the sunset
beyond the five yellow gums
at the war memorial.
Somewhere, blossoms, invisible.

Carnies bolt around the showground,
goey-run, prepping rides and pickup lines.
A hip-high carousel, a small ferris wheel.
The grandstand's shadow drenches the oval.

First thing this morning
a heron tall among the reeds and grass,
its careful measure a slow waltz with prey
as I cook up the coffee.

My voltaren and coke on the high verandah.
Holidays with my own grandparents fade
into sciatica's bright flare
in the dark by the hushing creek.

Wisteria

Christmas again at Wangi Caravan Park,
but the last one. None of us ever go back.
Grandad's leaning against the awning pole,
squinting across at Swansea, Nords Wharf,
Belmont, their windows bright pricks all summer.
Around the point, the lake spills with herons,
silver gulls, magpies, where we can almost make out
Bill Dobell hunched over, tending his wisteria.

Paterson Rd

Willows along the narrow road to Paterson
darken the creek called a river. A few birds
follow insects we can't see. Flowers hum with pollen
before they drop into the collapsing bank.

Birds

Birds spill out from the north,
shadows brief across changing trees.
The ridge's grief: where
could it begin to begin?

Walking home

No one else on this back road
staked down by trees stinking of wet ash.

Hills crackle with dawn – birdsong,
and the early light seems to hum.

The lake my family lived by's somewhere behind,
and the valley's folds open out past dawn.

My life was mine only once I left. Nostalgia drifts by
on this creek like a slick dropped from a burnout.

Past Cowan

This road through the hills goes
on and goes on. We stop
every second town. My friends

are stashed in country graveyards.
The trees here drain the earth
and shush water as it overs the rocks.

A black-shouldered kite hovers –
its whistle scrapes the hillsides.
The long island's in mist, though

the scent of marsh and the sound
of its birds rises to the ridgeline.
Casuarina needles soften the damp edge.

The narrow path
he broken water below
's gathered again.

Summer rides on

After Tao Qian

Summer rides on months longer, and then
the valleys, wiped with mist, beckon east
and rephrase the arms of water below. Ridge-top trees
grow scrawny from the weather – Ku ring gai's

spine claps birdsong to bursting stone and dropped
height, to shape a melody that curves and climbs
with the Old Pacific Highway. Fire trails and dusty
access roads fall or lift away, dry pollen on the wind.

After Han Shan

1.

This bedsit is home to a country boy.
Buses or cabs rarely drop passengers off:
the street-side trees so still that crows roost here,
the gutter full of cigarette butts and used frangers.

I go chocolate shopping on my own,
smoke joints in the park with my girlfriend.
And in this little flat? Books piled high
on my bedside table with the Chinese landscape print.

2.

Well, here we are, miserable academics,
starved of recognition, cold-shouldered.
No essays to write, and we've got only these poems –
scratch them or scrawl them, our minds frazzle.

Fark, who'd read this shit?
Actually, don't even worry about it –
we could spell out our poems in dog food
and even a stray mongrel would turn up its nose.

3.

I slaved my arse off over Joyce,
poring stupidly over *Finnegan's Wake*.
I'll be checking bookshop stock figures til I'm 80 –
a mong scribbling away at invoices and returns.

When I ask the I Ching, it says, *Look out* –
my life's dictated by bad fortunes told.
If only I was like the river red gums,
a pale shade of green even in drought.

4.

I was born more than forty years ago.
Ten thousand or more miles, I've been driven,
alongside rivers thick with willows,
across the reddened border with South Australia.

I drank Jim Beam in hope of acceptance,
read the poets, and Manning Clark's *History*.
But now, I'm back here in Kurri, head
on an old pillow, washing my ears out with home.

5.

Last year, when I was so poor,
I counted money for cretinous brothers,
I decided to work for myself
digging out gems among unpolished turds.

A smiling foreign critic wrote to me
and wanted to laud me in his *Review*.
I offered him only what I could,
You can't afford poems like these.

6.

My mind's like the moon's reflection,
crisply outlined on the choppy ocean.
Actually, that analogy's shit.
I don't have a clue what I'm saying.

7.

I'm pushing my mountain bike through Neath,
my empty hometown is just depressing.
Abandoned water board buildings,
ripped up pit railways.

My shadow wobbles and spins.
Even the servo is silent.
All those who ever lived here:
even the *Cessnock Advertiser*'s forgotten them.

8.

Low mist through the dawn streets.
Below, the Hawkesbury always leaves and returns.
From the Angler's Rest you hear an old
fisherman humming and singing Bob Dylan,

verse after verse after verse. I can't
stand it, all these cracked honey melodies.
*Dear Landlord, I won't underestimate
you, if you won't underestimate me.*

9.

I'm a heart-sore ring-in, in these mountains,
whinging about the floating seasons.
Picking at all these mushrooms and herb:
will it really make me enlightened?

The bush at my back door scrolls open —
the moon brushes off those thin clouds.
Should I go home to the Hunter
if the magpies and ghost gums keep me here?

10.

Another brilliant John Leonard Press book!
I'm overflowing with cleanskin red.
There: a currawong feeding its young —
I sit on the bench and just watch.

At home, there's rising damp.
The moon flows through my broken window.
Moments like these, I've got no minties,
so I'll read poems not published in Melbourne.

11.

When a bookshop proprietor read my poems,
he was lost — but sniggered and was queasy.
Writers Festival attendees at my reading
tell me my poems are very meaningful.

The members of my workshop
read them gob-smacked and enthralled.
But Les Murray read my translations
and knew he'd finally met with genius.

12.

If you've got the *Kurri Kurri Book of the Dead*
you don't need the Bible or Shakespeare.
Pull it from your dusty shelves
and flip through it from time to time.

After Li Bai

In Abermain, I find nothing

emptied coal cars bicker and howl
through Loxford

water drains below
where I walk
                jasmine?

the Sandemans' goat
deep in yard grass

midday   Deep Creek,
Abermain —
            (no
Buddhists!)

(the railway raised above
and split the town it owned)

where does it begin?
that paddock of slush? —

no family here anymore
my old church   the doctor's rooms,
a scout hall   where I wept once.
the quarry   a house past there.

that's enough   isn't it?

My father drives north all night, past the ferry

Past the slow brown river, its arms climbing
to reach past Wiseman's, St Alban's, Bucketty, Laguna,

towards Wollombi. The Macdonald creases its hills, thins, then,
and tightens. It peters to a spring, the road leashed close

above. Moon's through the gaps there, heaving
and bright, dispersing rag cloud and sheer country dark.

This shitty road trickles me near enough to home – smell of dust
and dry sclerophyll, a car that curls and winds all night.

Heading south

A grateful exile, I hit it downhill past Pelaw Main,
headed south but nowhere in mind. Flicking
between stations past the Brunkerville Gap,
I catch the fade-out of *A Little Ray of Sunshine*.

After Bai Juyi

Newcastle Cemetery, Sandgate

The Hunter drifts unseen
past Sandgate Cemetery

where my father's mother lies —
its mangroves beside the highway,

the roots finger in the mud.
In time the water table will return,

wash up and over and reclaim the dead.
The earthquake drummed out

its immense vowel. Some headstones cracked,
graves sunk a little deeper into the loam.

Waves sifting sand

1.

Just off Caves Beach sandbanks fall and rise.
Under the shifting sun, the tides turn cloudy

with fine sand forever, eating away at the lake,
the sea, the scarp and the ranges.

2.

The swell out past Blacksmiths is vicious and white,
jagged pearl. Sand sweeps up in there, always.

How could we think it would stop? Winter slides
out from the ocean, salt and kelp-rot on the shop awning.

3.

At Wangi the Patersons Curse is a curse.
Rain falls through the lakeside melaleuca

as your grief still breathes fog. There – Swansea.
Waves against the jetty, wind sings across the tinnies.

5.

Soon enough, Pulbah Island will be silty muck,
or the lake floor a trail of hills. An old photo

of your grandparents, so young, somewhere near here,
with war elsewhere. Did they imagine dying, so long apart?

From the provinces

From the provinces

Du Fu at Middle Harbour Creek

On the opposite bank a sacred kingfisher
gathers light – clear creekwater

turns sandy brown; the banksias,
bloodwood and ti-trees smell of invisible

blossom. My shoes the colour of coal dust
damp with a misjudged crossing.

There's a heron's cry over the slim and shaded
creek elbow, it fades and swims.

Han Shan drives through Campsie

You know, really, just fuck this shit.
Ensconced up past Leura fifteen hundred years,
and, first trip back on Beamish Street for vittles,
there's this poster – KFC wants to END HUNGER

Meng Haoran and the Hawkesbury Panther

The season's first rash of flies, a couple
of lambs born wrong. Creeks, parched all year,
sink under floods. Something dark crossed the road
just then – a black dog, or a cat the size of a dog.

Driving to Canberra with Du Fu

It's night now, we left in a hurry.
On the blank M7 taillights wander –
campfires, pyres, villages burning.
Du Fu asks, "How's your civil war

going?", assuming every country
's got one. "Nothing civil about it,
though we've offshored the body
count. Runs well in the marginals".

"Yeah, I read the dailies and wipe them.
The Emperor wouldn't allow that depth
of dishonour. These courtiers would be
lucky to flee as exiles, if, that is,

if their heads remained". "I think I like
the sound of your emperor". "Yes",
quizzically, "he is very loud". Signs fling by.
The freeway hisses, the petrol burns.

Li Bai at the Sandringham

I've never declined the offer of wine but
the house red here is sharper than a Mosman
punk's mohawk. Roaring Jack bounce the stage.
The bar's a horseshoe, and aglow with sweat.

Meng Jiao at the Lime Spiders, Fanny's, 1988

Paid the eight buck cover charge and shoulder through
to the back. Lost myself in the riffing bark and howl –
thousands of gibbons shrieking: they line
the whitewater hiss of the gorges all this Bicentennial year

Du Fu to Li Bai at Wallsend Cemetery

Here the city's edge falls off
toward the Hexham wetlands.

Once, a railroad curled
across where this town ends

to find a clutch of hill-shaded mines.
You're not to be found, but your grave,

my friend, if there is one, takes
a vast divot from the world.

Sun always falls here. Winter, and on this rise
the rainless earth dries and splits.

Summer appalls. This country needs something.
Water? A new dynasty? Money? Poems?

Notes

These poems are adapted, often very loosely indeed, from the poems below:

Windfall

Rainfall: John Burnside, "Rain", *The Hunt in the Forest*.

Robert Adamson in *The Valley of Gwangi*. "The final solstice", *Swamp Riddles*, and the film, *The Valley of Gwangi*.

Windfall: Caroline Caddy, "Donation" and "Submission", *Editing the moon*.

They Almost Belong: Sarah Holland-Batt, *The Hazards*.

At Night, driving: "Night Drive", Derek Mahon, *Selected Poems*.

At Seven Mile Beach: Chase Twichell, "The Whirlpool", *Ghost of Eden*.

Poems the size of Les Murray: Les Murray, "An Absolutely Ordinary Rainbow".

Sprung: "The last spring", Gig Ryan, *New and Selected Poems*.

The Kurri Kurri Book of the Dead: Charles Wright, "The Appalachian Book of the Dead" poems, *Black Zodiac* and *Appalachia*. Paul Kelly, *"Before Too Long"* and *"To Her Door"*; Deep Purple, "Smoke on the Water".

On looking into Pam Brown's *Selected*: Pamela Brown, *Selected Poems*.

Late, romantic: Rainer Maria Rilke, "Archaic Torso of Apollo".

Table: Rosemary Dobson, "The Continuance of Poetry: 7. Translations under the trees", *The Three Fates*.

Childhood Trauma: John Tranter, "Crying in Early Infancy":

"They burn the radio, they listen to the blue": no. 5.

"The automobile industry makes sense", no. 26.

"The drunk swindler falls from the bus", no.32.

"We laugh at ourselves with some difficulty", no.40.

"The woman falls in love's slow reduction", no.72.

"Does being the subject", no.68.

"The edge of the afternoon returns", no.62.

"They are courageous, even if it is induced", no.31.

Kurri 1977: J. S. Harry, "Griffith 1977", *New and Selected Poems*.
Wheelbarrow Variations: William Carlos Williams, "The red
wheelbarrow", *Spring and all*; and A. R. Ammons, *Tape for the Turn
of the Year*, p.71.
Hey, Bill is: Hey, Bill: William Carlos Williams, "This is just to say",
Selected Poems.
Edge: Bruce Beaver, "On the Edge", *Charmed Lives*.
Into evening: Simon West, "To the Morning's Gods", *The Ladder*.
White-faced heron: The Herons, Judith Beveridge, *The Domesticity
of Giraffes*.
Utterance: Tracy Ryan, "Confluence", *Scar Revision*.

Cockle Creek
Du Fu Variations:

On the *Narrabeen*, thinking of Aus Lit: "At Sky's end, thinking
of Li Po", translated by David Hinton, *The Selected Poems of Tu
Fu,*; and "Thoughts of Li Po from the World's End", John Hawkes,
A little primer of Tu Fu,.

Dreaming of Li Bai: "Dreaming of Li Po", David Hinton, *Tu Fu
Selected Poems*.

Spring scene: "Spring Scene", John Hawkes, *A little primer of Tu
Fu*; "Spring Scene" David Young, *Du Fu: A life in poetry*.

Traveling, late at night: "Thoughts, traveling at night", David
Hinton, *Tu Fu Selected Poems*.

Six variations: "Six quatrains", David Hinton, *Tu Fu Selected
Poems*.

Spring night: "Spring night in the Imperial Chancellery", *A little
primer of Tu Fu*.

The moon above my brother: "Moonlit night thinking of my
brothers", David Hinton, *Tu Fu Selected Poems*; "On a Moonlit
Night", John Hawkes, *A little primer of Tu Fu*.

Thinking of my son: "Thinking of my son", David Young, *Du
Fu: a life in poetry*; "Thinking of my little boy", David Hinton, *Tu
Fu Selected Poems*.

The same moon: "Moonlit night", David Young, *Du Fu: a life in poetry*.

Driving along Canterbury Road toward Milperra: "Looking out at the plain", David Young, *Du Fu: a life in poetry*.

Eucalypts along the Cooks River: "Alone, looking for blossoms along the river", David Hinton, *Tu Fu Selected Poems*.

Sting: "Spring", David Young, *Du Fu: a life in poetry*.

Drunks: William Hung, *Tu Fu: China's Greatest Poet*, p. 82, stanza 3.

Mines: "Traveling Northward", Kenneth Rexroth, from Eliot Weinberger, ed., *The New Directions Anthology of Classical Chinese poetry*.

Bridges: "Song of the War Carts", David Young, *Du Fu: a life in poetry*, p.43.

The front arrives: "Serving at the Front" David Young, *Du Fu: a life in poetry*, p.46.

North: from "The Journey North", William Hung, *Tu Fu: China's Greatest Poet*; from "The Journey North", David Hinton, *Tu Fu Selected Poems*; from "The Journey North", David Young, *Du Fu: a life in poetry*.

What got seen: "A view of the wilderness", Walter Bynner, retrieved from http://wengu.tartarie.com/wg/wengu.hp?l=Tangshi&no=184

Summer rides on: "Turning seasons", David Hinton, *The selected poems of T'ao Ch'ien*.

Uprising: *Laughing Lost in the Mountains: Poems of Wang Wei*, translated by Tony Barnstone, Willis Barnstone and Xu Haixin:

"The Mountain Dwelling of Official Wei", p.56

"For Someone Far Away", p.86

"Weeping for Meng Haoran", p.88

"For Scholar Pei in Fun after Hearing Him Chant a Poem", p.89

"Saying Goodbye to Spring", p.99

"The Emperor Commands a Poem be Written and Sent to my Friend, the Prefect Wei Xi", p.54

"West Long Mountain", p.75

"Seeing Zu Off at Qizhou", p.79

Cockle Creek:

Wang Wei's Wang River sequence: "Wheel-Rim River", David Hinton, *The selected poems of Wang Wei*; "The Wang River Sequence", G. W. Robinson, *Wang Wei: Poems*; Chang Yin-nan and Lewis C. Walmsley, *Poems by Wang Wei*.

Cockle Creek coda: "On returning to Wheel-Rim River", David Hinton, *The selected poems of Wang Wei*.

After Wang Wei:

1: "Deer Park", David Hinton, *The selected poems of Wang Wei*. Translations of this poem are explored in *19 ways of looking at Wang Wei*, edited by Eliot Weinberger and Octavio Paz.

2: Irving Yucheng Lo, *Sunflower Splendor*.

3: Chang Yin-nan and Lewis C. Walmsley, *Poems by Wang Wei*.

Berry, David Young, *Five T'ang Poets*, Wang Wei, p27

Adapted from *Laughing Lost in the Mountains: Poems of Wang Wei*, translated by Tony   Barnstone, Willis Barnstone and Xu Haixin:

Wisteria, "Living Lazily by the Wang River", p.33

Paterson Rd, "Going to the Country in the Spring", p.12

Birds, "Huazi Hill", p.27

Walking home, "Sailing at Night Beyond Jinkou Dike", p.92

Past Cowan, "From Desan Pass, Going Through Shaggy Forests and Dense Bamboo, Climbing Paths Winding for Forty or Fifty Miles to Yellow Ox Peak Where I See Yellow Flower River Shining", p.9

After Li Bai:

In Abermain, I find nothing: "High in the mountains, I fail to find the wise man", David Young, *Five T'ang Poets*. The italicized quote is Young's line.

My father drives north at night, past the ferry: "At Ching-Men Ferry, a farewell", David Hinton, *The selected poems of Li Po*.

Drinking: "Drinking together", William Carlos Williams in *The*

New Directions anthology of Classical Chinese poetry; "Drinking in the mountains with a recluse", David Hinton, *The selected poems of Li Po.*

Heading south: "Drinking with Shih Lang-Chun, I hear a flute on Yellow-Crane tower sing", David Hinton, *The selected poems of Li Po.*

After Bai Juyi:

Newcastle Cemetery, Sandgate: "At the Tomb of Li Bai", translated by Anthony Piccione and Caro Zhogong Chang http://poetrychina. net/wp/poets/pochui/5

Waves sifting sand: "Waves sifting sand", David Hinton, *The selected poems of Po Chu-I.*

The "From the provinces" book in this collection is hugely indebted to English language translators of the work of the classical Chinese poets, in particular David Young, David Hinton, Tony Barnstone, Willis Barnstone and Xu Haixin, and Burton Watson.

Acknowledgements

Some of these poems have been previously published in *Cordite*, *Guide to Sydney Rivers* (ed., Les Wicks), *Mascara*, *Meanjin*, *past simple*, *A Slow Combusting Hymn* (ed., Kit Kelen and Jean Kent) and *Southerly*. Many thanks to the editors.

The poems in "After Han Shan" was published in the Flying Islands chapbook, *After Han Shan* (2012). Many thanks to Kit Kelen for his permission to republish this sequence.

My gratitude goes out to the members of my erstwhile writing group: Adam Aitken, Liz Allen, Bonny Cassidy, Brook Emery, Jane Gibian, Mark Mahemoff, Niobe Syme, Lindsay Tuggle, Adrian Wiggins, Fiona Wright.

Thanks also to poets, friends, encouragers and early readers of some of these poems: Judith Beveridge, Pam Brown, Nathan Curnow, Lachlan Brown, Michelle Weisz, and to David Musgrave for his work, perseverance, energy and, by gosh, vision as an editor and publisher, and as a supporter of many poets.

This book is for Inez and Frankie.

www.ingramcontent.com/pod-product-compliance
Lightning Source LLC
Chambersburg PA
CBHW031000090426
42737CB00007B/617